W9-BHU-334

SUMMER

SEASONS OF THE YEAR

by Harriet Brundle

WINDMILL BOOKS

New York

SEASONS OF THE YEAR

Published in 2018 by **Windmill Books,** an Imprint of Rosen Publishing
29 East 21st Street, New York, NY 10010

Written by: Harriet Brundle
Edited by: Gemma McMullen
Designed by: Ian McMullen

Photo credits: Abbreviations: l-left, r-right, b-bottom, t-top, c-center, m-middle. All images are courtesy of Shutterstock.com. Front Cover, 5 – Sunny studio. 1 – vvvita. 2, 4lc – djgis. 3, 22bl – Andrey_Kuzmin. 4l Konstanttin. 4rc – Smileus. 4r – Triff. 6 – JonesHon. 7 – Zurijeta. 8 – BlueOrange Studio. 9 – mangostock. 10 – www.BillionPhotos.com. 11 – Serg64. 11bl,c – Evgeniy Ayupov. 11br - ips. 12 – Dudarev Mikhail. 13 – Subbotina Anna. 13tr – J. Marijs. 14 – Patrick Foto. 15 – Lucian Coman. 16 – gorillaimages 16inset – Valentyn Volkov. 17 – Sunny Forest. 17inset – Monkey Business Images. 18 – Olesia Bilkei. 19 – JaySi. 20 – iofoto. 21 – gpointstudio. 22r – Denphumi. 23bl – Ilya Andriyanov. 23inset – Mykola Mazuryk.

Cataloging-in-Publication Data
Names: Brundle, Harriet.
Title: Summer / Harriet Brundle.
Description: New York : Windmill Books, 2018. | Series: Seasons of the year | Includes index.
Identifiers: ISBN 9781499484151 (pbk.) | ISBN 9781499484038 (library bound) | ISBN 9781499483956 (6 pack)
Subjects: LCSH: Summer--Juvenile literature. | Seasons--Juvenile literature.
Classification: LCC QB637.6 B78 2017 | DDC 508.2--dc23

Manufactured in China
CPSIA Compliance Information: Batch #BS17WM: For Further Information contact
Rosen Publishing, New York, New York at 1-800-237-9932

Contents

Words that appear in **bold** can be found in the glossary on page 24.

Seasons of the Year

4

There are four seasons in a year. The seasons are called spring, summer, fall, and winter.

Each season is different. This book will tell you about summer!

5

Summer

Summer comes after spring and before fall. The summer months are June, July, August, and September.

January						
Sun	Mon	Tue	Wed	Thu	Fri	Sat
1	2	3	4	5	6	7
8	9	10	11	12	13	14
15	16	17	18	19	20	21
22	23	24	25	26	27	28
29	30	31				

February						
Sun	Mon	Tue	Wed	Thu	Fri	Sat
			1	2	3	4
5	6	7	8	9	10	11
12	13	14	15	16	17	18
19	20	21	22	23	24	25
26	27	28	29			

March						
Sun	Mon	Tue	Wed	Thu	Fri	Sat
				1	2	3
4	5	6	7	8	9	10
11	12	13	14	15	16	17
18	19	20	21	22	23	24
25	26	27	28	29	30	31

April						
Sun	Mon	Tue	Wed	Thu	Fri	Sat
1	2	3	4	5	6	7
8	9	10	11	12	13	14
15	16	17	18	19	20	21
22	23	24	25	26	27	28
29	30					

May						
Sun	Mon	Tue	Wed	Thu	Fri	Sat
		1	2	3	4	5
6	7	8	9	10	11	12
13	14	15	16	17	18	19
20	21	22	23	24	25	26
27	28	29	30	31		

June						
Sun	Mon	Tue	Wed	Thu	Fri	Sat
					1	2
3	4	5	6	7	8	9
10	11	12	13	14	15	16
17	18	19	20	21	22	23
24	25	26	27	28	29	30

July						
Sun	Mon	Tue	Wed	Thu	Fri	Sat
1	2	3	4	5	6	7
8	9	10	11	12	13	14
15	16	17	18	19	20	21
22	23	24	25	26	27	28
29	30	31				

August						
Sun	Mon	Tue	Wed	Thu	Fri	Sat
			1	2	3	4
5	6	7	8	9	10	11
12	13	14	15	16	17	18
19	20	21	22	23	24	25
26	27	28	29	30	31	

September						
Sun	Mon	Tue	Wed	Thu	Fri	Sat
						1
2	3	4	5	6	7	8
9	10	11	12	13	14	15
16	17	18	19	20	21	22
23	24	25	26	27	28	29
30						

October						
Sun	Mon	Tue	Wed	Thu	Fri	Sat

November						
Sun	Mon	Tue	Wed	Thu	Fri	Sat

December						
Sun	Mon	Tue	Wed	Thu	Fri	Sat

In the summertime, there are more hours of sunlight each day than in any other season.

The Weather

The sun shines in the summer.
The weather feels warm and dry.

We must be careful in the sunshine not to burn our skin.

Don't forget your sunscreen!

9

In the Backyard

We can play in
the backyard when
the weather is warm.

10

There are lots of insects in the backyard in the summer.

Which of these have you seen before?

Bee

Ant

Spider

Plants

Sunshine helps plants to grow. The flowers are colorful and the grass is green.

12

We must give the plants in the garden **extra** water in the summertime because there is less rain.

13

Animals

Animals are growing in the summer. Some eat green grass so they can grow bigger.

Animals must eat while there is lots of food. There is less food for them in the colder seasons.

Food

Lots of types of food grow in the summer. Apples and plums grow on the trees.

Apples

Plums

16

The fields are full of corn.
We use corn to make
breakfast cereals.

17

What Do We Wear in the Summer?

Hat

In the summertime we wear shorts and T-shirts because we want to stay cool.

T-shirt

Shorts

Don't forget your hat to **protect** your head from the sun.

18

It is fun to go to the beach. We wear swimsuits so we can go swimming.

Things to Do in the Summer

What would you take on your picnic?

It is fun to go on a picnic in the sunshine.

When the weather is sunny, it is exciting to go to the park.

Summer Fun

Draw a picture of something you enjoy doing in the summertime.

It might be you eating ice cream!

Did you know?

In places called **deserts**, the weather is sunny all year round.

Be careful not to look at the sun, even if you are wearing sunglasses. It will hurt your eyes!

23

Glossary

Desert: a place that is hot and does not get a lot of rain.

Extra: more than usual.

Protect: to look after or cover.

Index